CHIMERA

Carol Frost

· · · · · · · · · · · · · · · · ·

CHIMERA

CAROL FROST

PEREGRINE SMITH BOOKS
SALT LAKE CITY

First edition

93 92 91 90   5 4 3 2 1

Copyright © 1990 by Gibbs Smith, Publisher
All rights reserved; no portion of this book may be
reproduced in any manner whatsoever without written
permission from the publisher

Published by Gibbs Smith, Publisher, Peregrine Smith
Books, P.O. Box 667, Layton, Ut 84041, (801) 544-9800

This is a Peregrine Smith Book

Design by Randall Smith Associates

Back cover photo by Larry Mirachi

Printed and bound in the United States of America

Library of Congress Cataloging-in-Publication Data

Frost, Carol, 1948-
   Chimera / Carol Frost.
      p.   cm.
   ISBN 0-87905-370-4 : $9.95
   I. Title.
PS3556.R596C49   1990
811'.54—dc20   89-25570
                                                              CIP

The paper used in this publication meets the minimum
requirements of American National Standard for Infor-
mation Sciences—Permanence of Paper for Printed
Library Materials, ANSI Z39.48-1984 ∞

ACKNOWLEDGMENTS

These poems, sometimes in earlier versions, appeared in the following publications:

American Poetry Review: "Apple Rind."
The Antioch Review: "The Landscapes."
Crazyhorse: "Eating the Whole."
Denver Quarterly: "Nature Morte."
The Gettysburg Review: "Icarus in Winter," "This Early."
The Georgia Review: "Alto," "Harriet Street."
Ironwood: "Chimera," "Genesis, Rodin's," "Sunfish," "Wild Partridge," "Winter Poem."
The Journal: "Child Frightened by a Monkey," "Puppet Master."
New England Review and Bread Loaf Quarterly: "Dynasty 1989," "Roadside Shrine."
Pacific Review: "Folio."
Ploughshares: "Acorns," "In Scarecrow's Garden."
Poetry Northwest: "A Butterfly and a Day," "After Byzantium."
Prairie Schooner: "A Field Full of Black Cats," "Apple Rind," "Music for Death," "Ode to the Horseshoe Crab," "The Beautiful Islands," "The Table Garden," "Root."
Seneca Review: "The King's First Soliloquy."
William and Mary Review: "Skinny Dipping."

The author wishes to thank the editors of these periodicals and to add special acknowledgment to Ion Books for permission to reprint three of the poems in this collection that first appeared in *Day of the Body*.

She also wishes to thank the Hartwick College Board of Trustees for a summer grant, during which several of these poems were written.

FOR MY HUSBAND
AND MY SONS

CONTENTS

· · · · · · · · · · · · · · · · · · ·

WINTER POEM

Far past the broken walls, slashed stumps,
homeward or homeless, the black birds
in long purple streaking cling
to the undefinable bulge of the world.

And again I am in winter,
walking across the bronzed marshes
where as a child I went alone to skate.

The branches and hedges held a strange transparency,
as though, at the fall of leaf,
a wall of green twilight reared against them;
and the pond accrued a green and stony glow.

The log on the edge of the pond,
the snow-covered rocks, and the frightened birds
seemed as much laden with deep breath as myself—

the soft thudding sound as I tromped
through the green twilight and the snow
enriched with deer-tall, quill, the sunk solids
of the earthbound.
                    I skated easily,
a part of winter, unknowing, like Bruegel's skaters,
black comedians who seem in their blackness

to be keeping watch over the whiteness of space;
like magpies; all of us dipping our wings
in the green twilight, verging
on the vacancy in which we have no place.

I.

CHIMERA

CHIMERA
. . . .

By the verge of the sea a man finds a gelatinous creature,
parching, thick as a shoe, its head a doubtful dark green
that leans toward him as he bends near in some dark
wonderment of his own. The sky is haunted by pure light,

the sea a rough mixture of blue, and green, and black.
     Suddenly
he hears the air rent with loud cries and looks to see
pelicans on the piers raising their wings then falling,
          changing shape
to dive into the sea. He thinks of Bosch's rebellious angels
changing shape as they are pursued out of the immaculate sky.

Who are they? Angels who accept the hideous
and monstrous. Fallen, they make up a nightmare fauna.
Say the sea is to be questioned. Below the bounds
of this estate, through rainbowed cold, the rockheaded and
          cored

of bone, the chimera our madness does not cease to reinvent
and which we dare not think alive, crawls in a thick ooze.
Yet even this one, torn to the plain insides and leaking dyes,
exudes a gentle unrest of the soul. Is it not good? The man
          pauses,
looks around—the sea undulates, sharpening and smoothing

all the grooves that history has graven on the sand—
then he puts his hands under the terrible flesh and heaves it
as far as he can back into the Atlantic, as if it were the mirror
of a lost estate, the dawn-time of the world's first season.

SUNFISH

• •

Vertebrate, kin to the fully armed form
sprung upon the earth like Athena
from the head of Zeus, how is it no love

or scruples are stirred as you flap
at the end of my line, foul-hooked,
glistening? I recapitulate your gill slits

yet can't make of the life history of fish
a lesson, someone's first flounder
resurrected from a shallow grave,

water sparkling with green points of reflection
like tiny mirrors when green fry
swim out of their scales in fright.

There are no inhibitions, moments of hesitation,
no book of pain borne in your mind
when crawfish with lines tied to them

appear in the pond, and your muscleless face
is a mask the angler cannot pity.
I have held you—spinous, slimy,

and fragrant as dead leaves—in my bare hands
to admire your aegis of blue-greens
and yellows shading into one another

as if formed by sunbeams through a shower,
and moments later pulled out your air bladder
with the hook. So naturally was death wrought,

I felt no evil, and so glorious the colors
lying on the surface of the water
robbed of moral.

NATURE MORTE

. . . .

Two rigid bodies
of fish, brown cut-glass skin,
nudge the land's edge
as if to nudge us and stun
gluttony to a dumb repose.

Two bodies, I said,
but only one head,
as if the smaller, as good as bait,
had gone begging too near
the larger maw.

Feeding both mouths,
the feast began,
and from their depth they rose
lashing their tails,
exiles

from the gentle rigors of water,
now landed There's the gorged
look. There's the dark intestine
in the jaw of the other,
and no sleeping off the meal.

No formation of angels,
no words, finally,
for the error and virulence
when two cravings
meet head on.

ODE TO THE HORSESHOE CRAB

Dullest of all creatures, the horseshoe crab
crawls with its brethren to the beach at low tide;
they are broad-backed with muck-colored plates
and out of water look like stones.

Boys who wouldn't torture anything higher,
torture these crabs, which have nothing
that could be called real eyes, their blank backs
suggesting the faces of idiots.

They have no enthusiasms, and can't move fast.
Their undersides are full of twiddling legs
and leaf-like gills. *Limulus polyphemus*
has a low sex drive.

Commonly, boys crack the crabs with stones,
large ones that the back can't bear,
and something that looks like brains,
a gray tapioca that smells sweet, comes out.

Having no capacity for love or thought,
they trudge in the salty tide, swallowing small forms
of marine life. In 350 million years the sun
has failed to break their sleep, their sleep before being born.

GENESIS, RODIN'S

Stayed, serpentine in mud,
the figure lifts without muscular energy
from the mineral floor blindly
to try to stand under his own power;

and in his forever
making himself, full-nerved in the great lines
of the torso, oblivion thigh-high,
we see the declining daylight wrestle in the mud and weed.

No arms or feet, darknesses
crawling like grubs from under stones,
and still the ghost in the mind
understands itself, though cannot take its meaning

all at once: Of the imprisonment
we think of hydrocarbons faintly zooming
in their kingdom, and the unsettled visions,
like portals hung too high, of a god.

ROOT
. . . .

How can anyone refuse to answer the torturer's questions
about politics and principle
when the body's roots are exposed, except with hatred—
palpable as dirt, the tines of a pitchfork, stones, scattered lime,
and a slight green stem splitting the heart?

                               Even the intern snouting
through the chest with drainage tubes knows bodily hurt
isn't concerned with reasons and averts his eyes. Hate
grows solid, smelling faintly of ether of many evenings
and blood; rale-voiced; multiplying. Essays on faith have
    less power.
Without regard to season, death's blossom resurrects and
    resurrects.

CHILD FRIGHTENED BY A MONKEY
• • • • • • • • • • • • • • • • • • •

Tokugawa Period

Here, with palms raised and hooting, a monkey
walks toward a scared boy whom an adult lifts away.

They live in a drawing from Japan the uneasy life
we feel for them. The creature's gesture, so much like

our own, unwanted, seems to question our being
more than bodies with the heads of men. A monkey swung

down from the trees. All the ground was strange—
untrampled earth, boundless and flowing grains.

And then he was a man.
With chisels, paints, mottoes, and incised stone,

he recorded the terrifying and elegant animals
walking near him, like vessels

whose entrails are missing, wide mouths agape
as if bewailing their maker. To sketch his own face,

and later the boy's, took a thousand years,
a cloud of charcoal on nature's

resemblances: If the gaze in the eyes
looks like a young god struggling with fears,

the plane of the temples is closely the breadth
of the ape's, the parchment showing both.

what's left to draw or say? Ceremonial swords and dress
for the adults, a brown-pelted monkey on a leash

gesticulating, and the onlookers laughing
at the pathos of children, their faces crawling

with the faith of the ages,
hairless, not red like the monkey's.

The spirits that congealed these inks and moved
the artist's hands have wandered

long since to other pantheons,
yet return to tell of their ordeal with inhuman

forms and the way of bending nature
to dreams by looking, with eyes closed, in a mirror.

A FIELD FULL OF BLACK CATS

Cats in fields sit
still as idols
catching sunlight
catching moles.

Through the broken lattice-
work of grasses
they stare for hours, black
pelts burning.

One can imagine
in the belly
of each cat's shadow
a mole being

held in thrall, completely
taking the sun down
to earth, making
new terrain:

skies muscadine,
grass like tongues,
stones coughed-up
balls of fur.

Death is irremediable
here. There is no
reaching into the heart
of violence

when the cat paw sweeps
suddenly toward
the mole. The onyx
and yellow eyes

take the uptwisted flower
in as nothing
when the cats walk back
to porches

to lick themselves and drowse,
the hunched-up moles
having ended
in their hot mouths.

RED DEER

The red deer in summer sunlight
browses slowly in the landscape
we make of the forest. It is beautiful
and slays me with its delicacy,
its ankles. Bugs dance above the briars,
and fleshy raspberries are tinged black;
sun is falling. The Indians saw this contour
of land and the red deer,
stalking it through pines,
bits of brown like piles of little eggs
its trail to the river
where the last lights come.
Its bones and sinews sewed the shoes
for silence where I keep vigil now,
on the same ground, listening for a rustle
that is louder than the weight of birds
in the underbrush, wanting to see
the alarmed head turn, the large eyes.
I walk, and stop, and walk,
my body thinking, what does
the deer matter except it is flesh
and I have smelled it?
If I cut open the red coat,
I could live in it.
Green going gray going black,
I stand in violence, in death,
and I am happy—with the chill of fear.
The light withdraws; chills me; alters
nothing. At the root of humanness
a cup of blood
nature spills. And this is part
of everything I see or make or am.
I can hide it in a closet like a gun
to be shown in all its hiddenness
or paste it over with yellow, for sanctity,
and cool greens. But this once
let me tell the truth
that can't be told
outright. I had no pity.
The deer's last breath
crawled out like a clear beautiful ray
of sun on stones. I kissed
its head. I couldn't help myself.

THE KING'S FIRST SOLILOQUY

after the carving on the Tukulti Altar

This is the carving where deity withdrew:
a king shown twice, first standing
then kneeling before the empty throne of his God.

No king before in history
is ever on his knees. No scene before in history
indicates the growing puzzlement

as he moves forward and his forefinger
softly axes the empty air,
his face made mysteriously rich—as though

less by stone than by colors
laid on the surface of the carving
by the king's quietness, it is held together,

quietness already filling with distresses,
pleasures, aches, knowledges, and smells
to tell him he is.

It is a form
of suffering. And we are meant to understand
the whole past world leans against the king

as the story of himself wells up in him,
momentarily angelic, momentarily demonic—
the balance like a finger held in mid-air

then moved, the air changing by its passage.
For the king the question:
Why does my life say this to me?

And since the God approached
dissolves, he must imagine
what could not possibly be there,

scribbled at the edges of his mind,
like a sickness of the inner ear, a king alone
in a throne room talking to his own despair.

THE TUMORED ANGEL

The wings whir more slowly,
weary of holding him halfway between alabastrine
vacancy and a pile of hills. He thumps down hard,
humming a sarabande
he's been taught for materializing. His body's
in a sheet, no scrotum, no shoes.
Docile and radiant, he peers
into a trailer window at television
noise and the blue light, at people hiding,
it seems to him, from the cold glory
of fall's sunrise. They're looking at a soap opera.

It's the same story.
The angel is supposed to touch one of them
on the shoulder, these amateur believers,
and in a moment of recognition, like knowing the yelp of
        hounds
is geese, he or she will sense God's
mastery. This angel doesn't like
easy conversions; he too was a man
fluttering toward salvation, as a moth flutters
toward bright lights and destruction.

He changes from veil to flesh
and indicates the tumored hollows of himself
with the sign of the cross. If the believer
reaches in and touches gold, the promised
Paradise, as surely as lights go out, will disappear;
but feeling tumor, he will be reminded of all
the places, drawn quivering and cold,
that cannot be called good unless
someone reaches in and touches and is moved.

The angel squirms when touched (another ploy?)
and thinks of monks in hell; he pictures his insides
as lumps of dead roe and Time burning in coal
blue day. But in his face the heart's color comes,
in his earth-brown eyes the world.
Then he passes without word
through the diminishing sculptures of trees.
The smell of cold leaves scarcely names the event,
and the angel, knowing he is deathless, pauses
before the long climb zenithward, wanting to feel
upon his shoulders not wings, but the weight of the wind.

II.

THE
LANDSCAPES

THE LANDSCAPES

Watch them. The landscapes. That urge, glory
before the roar of each new surf; what goes on
before the plowman tames the jumbled hills
or points the wind. Move to the edge
of the room, let the others pass. No guide
will help you see. No dates or "middle periods."
It must be with the sense
of utter lonesomeness, yourself walking to the mountain
or lying under the pear tree's wild whites and viridians.
You look at a sunset sometimes,
and you know you've never seen it,
the quarry's living glare before bursting for cover.
Look now! Is something caught here? How to hold
creation in the eyes. How to savor,
before Eden made bestial and common glory
man's sorrow, the mountains, sea, hawk, leaf mold,
rotting bark. And no trace of anecdote.

A BUTTERFLY AND A DAY

Butterfly, as you hang on the knife-
edge of an iris leaf

needing nothing but the barest breaths
to send you along jubilant paths

one way or the other, plying
in the rippling heat your bright wings

with no dance in mind
and the water garden's diamonds

in the making light below,
so tomorrow

may for a brief moment catch,
as if on someone's final waking thought, then lurch

into morning. You are engendered
by the wind's first measure. You are a bird

too frail to have an equilibrium
and sing the song of random

forms cut out of air and light,
paring away waste, adding it,

on your paired wings. Past rest and motion,
dried skins, flaunting flowers in the garden,

you wander,
embowered in error:

So the day
toward horizons, in beauty

and chaos sails.

WILD PARTRIDGE

. . . .

The same bird over and over again,
quiet so long I had passed by,
drums from the last crisped leaves

up through the branches that had been fire.
Treading moss and stopping my breath,
I've gotten as close as to the russet brink

of an autumn sky and lost it
to the disheveled light. . .
a few wood berries, barley seed

under some pines, a liquid chuckling
somewhere ahead, then on the northern air—
beauty, autumn, vision burning

their overlapping images into dusk.
Can I stalk the wild partridge
and forget, seeing the fallen ash,

the leaves scattered and rotting,
how each moment soars, in truth,
in mortal surprise, away from us always?

THE TABLE GARDEN

• • • • • • • • • • • • • • • • • • •

Because it was made of fire spun to incredible thinness
and you gave it to me, I put it here in the table garden
when it broke, near the gnarled trees like bonsai,

the hand-tended hills and constant valleys.
It stands quietly as horses do
leaning on a boulder,

and the pliant green
tips of the trees shudder when the bowl of earth
is moved.

As translucent as the current on the branch,
the glass Pegasus seems to bloom

with the colors of wilderness, from within.

Crippled, awry, propped, nonetheless
it gives something to the garden nature cannot:

far beyond the fallen leaf,

whatever the heart in pieces can recollect
after the healing ends.

IN SCARECROW'S GARDEN

Loosely bound and buttoned on a pole, clothed in the
	gardener's cottons,
the scarecrow stretches as if to feign sleepiness, and
	sparrows
spurt from the garden beyond his sleeves. He swells
and soft green light invades the narrow rib, a space to fit a
	life in
but the breeze drops. It seems he needs only to catch a
	bird
and put it in his shirt, a birdheart to give the sensation of
	substance,
but he scares it away with his own little spurts
of freedom. Perhaps the thin cry in the raspberries is the
	bird's. Why?
Why do the scarecrow's gestures seem goodbyes that still
	want saying?
Yellow pulls across his wood shoulders, and his body
	shakes. So handled
by wind, he is life and hurt? Scarecrow, never mind
that you cannot get down and, shapeless, hang on your
	wooden backbone
like moth wings on a winter weed; it's spring.
The birds are back, ravenous but beautiful. The bulbs are
	opening.
You are not alone. That's what the tendrils of wind meant
livening your shirt. You are all motions the world makes,
the violence and sorrow, and the green leaves flowering at
	your feet.

DYNASTY, 1989

Like a tent of tapestries,
the green walls and roof sway

closely, little terrible flowers
bristle in the woolen air,

and a caravan of cutter ants
is traveling along the route

to the forbidden city and the queen,
bearing green gifts, green

banners. The wars, the necessary cannibalism
have slipped from memory, as have the names

of the enemy, in the single-minded dream
of returning home. What of the rumored schism

between castes, a change in rule?
Where paths are steep the mind levels,

and that is the world. The world is where
they are walking. By means of feelers

or with pats they invite one another for food,
for the way home and to work for common good.

THE BEAUTIFUL ISLANDS

In the tropics the houses sweat.
You learn to eat hot sauce
on beans and rice
and raw conch with a splash of lime,
drink the white rum of sunlight.
The basket market ignites
slowly in reds
and yellows.

Emerald, and jasper, and black, and olive,
the sea on coral breaks
its snowy parasols.
The sun's a lion shedding
imperial fur onto the clean dirt yards,
rolling in heat waves,
lasting after rain.

You shoulder the force of the sun
cutting cane.
You walk with George, the concessioneer,
who describes his beating
when he was young and cut his head
with a straight razor.
Under the tyranny

of sky mingling toward sea
you laugh along with George.
And onward, as school bells
descant their brilliant phrases.
In the interior
the sun consumes the floral bracts,
and shoreline waters shift sands over
the toes of the tourists.

PINEAPPLE

· ·

Green-shadowed venders sit, without a book or dominoes,
their children finger the pineapple spines
or play behind the wooden stands,
a bee sips a juicy rag, and the sun ferments
like a yellow vat in a warm room.

Patience and anticipation are allied,
are husks for the machete.

And those who pay their bolivars
taste summer and sugar-soaked fruit,
taste times's momentary laughter:
green, drunken, or ideal.

Those who cut the pineapple
return to their stillness like bowls.

ACORNS
· · · · · · · · · · · · · · · · · · ·

Last night some acorns fell
and woke me as they struck
the roof. Each acorn rolled,
a die cast down the shakes,

to tell my chances in
the sun and in the snow
to come. What might have been
a grief, I didn't go

to look for in the night.
I closed my eyes to sleep—
beneath the roof and oak,
and hidden stars that keep

their silver courses even
when foreverness of snow
glazes the window pane
with a cold brilliance so

it seems the world is frozen
in place. I told myself,
as plain as lettering
in almanacs each life

is marked by green and dying
seasons, and in the dead
of winter the stonecracking
wind over neighbor ground

is no surprise; nor spring
in the flash of a wing going
around a corner. Now
as ever, sweet dark slipping

through my fingers, time goes,
revolving like a door
between two worlds
we have to leave to enter.

THIS EARLY

This morning's wind-sleeves
flick the birch leaves, as if gravel
were lightly tossed into green-scummed water,
making holes. Now if ever might one notice the cult
of early summer, sweet carrion above ground
and masks of ants.
Gardeners look at the flowers. Yes, gold smears
the stamens inside plaited silks
too tender, this early,
to be touched. They look at the soil,
crude, granular, and its newly opened doors—
their flowers and spent time
as things die or move with new life
departing or coming through.

APPLE RIND

Someone else was afraid and spoke to me
and I couldn't answer . . . swallowing oxygen
from a tube. And then? The cool blade
freeing rind from an apple,
like the first touch of day. How long
I'd been in someone's still life—the blade
hidden, dividing—and was helpless.

Perfectly drugged, I lay just shy of winter
in my own mind. My cut chest felt nothing,
no terror, no pain. And there were morphine's sweet-
and-fruit boxes piled on the white terrain
like reasons for lives and death.
The orchard was weathered to admonitory bareness
except for a few frozen apples
above a disturbance of snow—the hoof prints
of deer coming by several routes to this late harvest,
the dim haunches and various limbs
afloat on movement that can break
or double back into the gray calm of woods.

How to explain directions a mind takes
or why I told no one how much I wanted
to come back to this beautiful, stupid world.

ROADSIDE SHRINE, SAN CRISTOBAL, VENEZUELA
. . . .

Out of the tropical light and into faith, a stone is found
     in a sugarcane field
by a man a month before his father-in-law lends him
     money
for a used Mack truck. That he felt luck in its smoothness
     gets around
and someone whose baby son coughs in his sleep
     touches it next.
When the child dies, the town learns you have to put
     more into it
than you feel at the time, and they build a small shrine,
patterning the altar with flowers, dressing a thin doll
in golden clothes.   In candle shadow,
I see the letters of thanks, pictures of healed persons and
     truck statues.
When was need so unambiguous? What is there to do
     here:
(a) lament my loss of simplicity, (b) probe the room as if
     a pattern
in what people left behind could subdue the force of
     light's
diminishment in the cane fields, (c) reflect that even if a
     longing
is satisfied, it doesn't matter a damn because of the death
I have held in my arms, (d) all of the above? That part of
     mind
always finding in one piece of luck its counterpart,
as with plenty, excess; beauty, dismemberment; love and
     life, absence.

SEAGULLS AND CHILDREN
● ● ● ● ● ● ● ● ● ● ● ● ● ● ● ● ● ● ●

I do not know how it is possible to walk through the
    landscape
at the time without asking questions: not the riddle
of egg and hen (the egg came first, for its essential
    features
in birds were present in reptiles from which birds
    descended),
or about how it was done, most birds lacking a penis,
but just thinking out loud that life here in the sunflat
    between inlet
and ocean seemed impossible. There were no sophistries
    in the sand,
nor in the continuing shrill and dive of the seagulls,
as we made our way to swim in the rougher water,
    running
from clumps of grass to the boards drifted in during
    winter's high tides,
beside the field of speckled eggs. The heat prickled
my salt-touched back; heat rose from the white kiln. Yet
    no distraction
broke my study the morning we kneeled by nest after
    nest
to see the yellow-soaked birds, skin, bone, and feathers.
There was only one way to look at them: unshell them,
and while calamity wheeled and cried above our heads,
we bloodied our fingers trying to get them dry and
    flying.
Five small figures by a cache of live and dead creatures—
seeing this now in the thin, bright glaze of the mind
like a gallery piece, what is lamented? What so possesses
    us?
I remember the size of beak relative to the head, and the
    lightness
of the bodies, then piece by piece reentering the world,
standing with our knees burnt from the salt-sand, the
    racking sun,
and swimming for hours, the rush of waves filling our
    eyes and ears.

WEB-MAKING
· ·

A spider sways along that wondrous slur,
its own silk, thrown from columbine to undiscovered
columbine, and when the cat's moony head
destroys the suspension, the spider
levitates to another flower to loop, in the quiet,
something like a line drawing of a constellation,
botanical, feeling with its 8 legs
for the tensile strength, as the mind plays with theorems.

Sometimes the spider, small as a fingertip, as a star
      beyond one's finger,
on its silk swing swings up high
and winks away.

To study the spider and its web-making
you need a random sample of many
and a delicate telescope to watch the garden, the
      columbine.
They habitually spin at night.
Dawns you can feel their wet, invisible lines
cross your skin. That's when you notice
the apparent chasms they must cross, and think the
      natural world
and the quantum heavens of crab, ram & bear
are as the Ancients saw them in the mind's eye,
pulled most delicately
together by silk inventions. What is a web?

Something time takes to finish, or to break
or to become the way things look in.

III.

MUSIC FOR
DEATH

ALTO

The day of chorus she was sent out
for singing wrong notes, for conceiving
herself a soprano, she stood in the hallway.
Behind the door voices braided Bartok
into garlands. She had never been so ashamed.
See the roses, blooming yonder,
far from dead leaves — she heard the words
and saw the soprano notes perched breathlessly
above the staff, the red and orange vapors
making melody. She'd sung with the tenors
when they had the melody.
                                        But now
she told herself this would be her lesson.
Outside the chorus room, the bottom
of the music brought her back, the darker voices,
she thought, like shadows in the song.
And though she listened for the unisons
as if for the meaning of a garden of roses,
when she went back into the room, the air
was filled only with the stale essence of their breath.

A CHILDHOOD MEMORY

A smoky autumn afternoon,
overcast. The children
have knives in their hands.
They are clashing quietly,

carefully, against the day's softness.
It is in the playroom. Cain's
forehead is unmarred.
Their bodies are light with feints,

jokes, and pride. The moments
simply pass through the room.
The father comes down the stairs.
He is in his bathrobe,

unshaved. He bellows,
his face creeping with the anger
of the house. For he doesn't know
what they do. What should they be without

the fight where they see themselves,
one running, one prone in a red stain?
The children have knives in their hands,
giggling, looking away from the man.

FOLIO

. . . .

I imagine the leaves dried butterflies,
autumn folded and hung up,
and the dampers closed before dusk
to keep the heat in the stove.
The days go leisurely down to sod,
frost making a clean cage
for next year's flowering. It is the folio
for the future; the garden gone
and come; stove ash, spoil heaps of table scraps,
and the green golden wings above the rows.

I walk by the boarded-up plate glass
and branded brick front of someone's home,
the drunk on the corner flashing
such thoughts of ruin that the raw estate
returns, colder and larger and more subject
to rage. So will we walk the landscape,
the furled leaf in the crevice
upholding the record,
the dawn a weak burning
above the canted walls?

ICARUS IN WINTER

If Breugel were wrong, and Icarus fell in the dead of the
    year,
freezing in the stratosphere that made his wings' wax
    brittle,
he fell here where a ball of suet hangs from a string

like a little low earth. How lonesome evening seems,
as if something felt part of itself missing.

The people indoors watching television, sitting in chairs,
seem never to come into the yard; they do not lament
the season's decrease. They only feed the few birds.

Where are yesterday's sparrows and wrens?
Above the branches of the oak,
washed in colors we feel but cannot find?

Swan-colored, ice-colored, rare-gas-and-light colored,
sounding to those indoors like a natural disaster—
a broken bough, a barn roof lost—Icarus

fell in this bare yard with no witness—no one
ploughing a field, no ship of state concerned with itself,
no evidence of suffering.

                These sightless walls
and shoveled entrances where no one comes,
even the white ground where Icarus is lying—

how sorrowless they make the landscape seem.
But no lie is made up entirely of lies,
and no one knows who feels what and how much,

sickening at spectacle, turning off the TV.
Beneath the snow are pieces of every summer, buds and
stunted roots so far below sense that they don't show.

AFTER BYZANTIUM
. . . .

They have it all. In congestion
around their front door, they have a motorcycle, power
mower, oil rings, transmission, wheels,
everything to make more than one pickup.
And even in freedom, with morning's gold leaf tile
touched askew to bathe the countryside in fire, they labor
as if in streets and alleys. Look at these slums,
the machined houses like packing crates
sprung around the county route, the signs
saying garages and body shops. Are they being
what they please? Once where dark, light, sound
took their own course, they are settling
down with their trash, their broken motors
sprung to life again, whirring and ticking
through the trees like goldsmiths' birds.

SKINNY DIPPING

The afternoon, ending, makes no sign,
but the crows and the warm wind which rake across
the thick pines fall away. In twilight that follows
we sit a long time by the green pool.
Is it the stress of quiet, a whirling in ourselves,
that makes us shed, one after the other,

our summer cottons like pupal skins
and slip into the cool water? Flushed limbs,
breasts, and ropy hair, we wrestle
within ourselves to be another, better, stronger,
less prone to hurts, then rise, wearing our towels
over our shoulders nowhere near like wings.

EATING THE WHOLE

• • • • • • • • • • • • • • • • •

mouse, first the cat sits off to one side,
perhaps reliving the crawl into deep grass
and snap of the neck. A spinning leaf

mesmerizes him. How it tastes,
the skull he crushes, and what
shared images of stealth are released

at that moment, I'd like to ask.
He softens each part with his teeth,
then swallows all, the soft fur and red

sinew holding together like a piece of clothing
in the mud. What use to say
that he washes his face with his paws

and that he looks beautifully
insolent? In the shiny spring air
he stretches in a spot of sunlight,

pricking his ears for the birds'
exciting minors, drowsing, not a mouse-
hair on the lawn, nor a guilty murmur.

AUTUMN APOLOGY

Already the land is starting to forget gardens.
The dew, no longer sweet, glazes the latticed woods
with an unreal brilliance,
so the eyes must be shielded.
Reminiscences no longer hold the heart completely,
as someone held me a little roughly
once in somber deep groves.
Gold and silver lacquers
can't jail leaves in trees or warmth in the air.
The touch I was utterly dissolute to,
that caused collapse behind my knees,
sunslides in the lake,
is unconjurable.
Bits of the world, leaves, songs
scatter in painted light.
The days
break.

HARRIET ST.

. . . .

The fadedness of stone
markers shows the wear
of weather. And hers,
long life near a yard of bone.

She's naked and weeds
her garden, and seems to stare at nothing.
The hot wind swings
its sharpened sickle where dark deeds

jumble with good, and begun
things end. The wing a vandal
lopped off from a stone angel
props itself on her porch in the sun.

This bears deep looking into,
all the appearances of madness
and death, or is it just coincidence,
the ancient crone, not dressed, the few

artifacts of grief
strewn on Harriet Street
across from the cemetery? In this heat
perfect connections of belief

come easily. But look.
All her dresses blow
on a clothesline. She may not bow
to earth from burdens, but to pluck

what spasms of flowers
and gems there are,
most sweet, most stolen, where
near to the living, graves are.

PUPPET MASTER

After the exact imitation of a living bird—
the quick motion of the bill
and just swelling of the throat—I wanted to make
something the sum of whose gestures
no one could make before: the limbs rose-amber,
formed like a boy's, the nose aquiline;
and lines of azure to signify the eyes under a brow
where springtime dreamed.

Then, through slow, galvanized thread,
motion I thought of as simple feeling
lifted him up and down, as when daffodils bob
in the garden. "Live," I said and again
"live." But his head knocked the wall, sideways.

What was he if magic made him
a boy? What was I to myself
if lying in scattered parts,
piece successively flying to piece,
I sat up, stood, and, capped by my skull, danced?

From elements less visible
than captive thread and clockwork, the habitants
of wood or flesh can lift their heads
in a way that says the world,
like the workshop, is all of theirs. Son, father,
Lazarus, lonely god, the dreamt shapes
rise in the sawdusty air, to touch
for a moment the little known of wonder.

MOZART

· · · · · · · · · · · · · · · · · · ·

The books say genius, prodigy.
This means so little. Or that he loved his canary
perched on the wire swing
to sing

its repertoire of linking trills.
It's not the music he wasn't to write, nor the still-
unspent longings that led
him to his deathbed

singing his Requiem, nor the pauper grave;
but when he put notes and staves
on music paper
as aria or prayer,

the softly boiling flames of spirit
that seems insubstantial, though we hear it,
were also caught there.
That he was here

at all, we fail to make sense of—
his trouble with women, his difficult love
for his father, his debts,
his death-

mask crumbling—except when we hear
his bits of song making architecture.
It's as though
a rococo

aviary were being built, with one bird
in mind, and it is liquid gold,
the intricate curving
bars proving

the singer is both held and free.
Such is his voice: a gust of melody
no one has known, flying yellow archangels
though all else falls.

MUSIC FOR DEATH

. . . .

You are right. At death I might well desire both day and
    rest,
some calm place where light is stabilized on an arbor,
a table, green glasses, and damask. The taste is of earth
    and sunlight,
tomatoes with folds at the blossom end and a large rough
    navel
with a bit of stem still attached, oil with basil
and lots of garlic, causing thirst for wine. And the music
to be played at my funeral must be the sound of the
    rosined bow
working against the wind, not old keys that are only
    echoes, but strange
gold in the beetle's click, a jay, a three color bird, a brown
    thrush,
their asides and intimations like the napkin songs
of great composers, written before the last bread and wine
    are gone.